Taoist Leadership
The Way of Subtle Influence

1st Ed

David Tuffley PhD

*The best leaders are those their people hardly know exist.
The next best is a leader who is loved and praised.
Next comes the one who is feared.
The worst one is the leader that is despised ...
The best leaders value their words and use them sparingly.
When they have accomplished their task,
the people say, "Amazing!
We did it, all by ourselves!
-- Lao Tzu*

Published 2024 by Altiora Publications
AltioraPublications.com/
ISBN-13: 9798509620287

Copyright 2024 David Tuffley and Altiora Publications.
All rights reserved. Without limiting the rights under copyright reserved above, no part of this publication may be reproduced, stored in, or introduced into a retrieval system, or transmitted, in any form without the written permission of the owner.

About the Author, David Tuffley PhD is a distinguished scholar of comparative religion and a dedicated follower of the Tao, bringing a unique blend of academic rigor and personal insight to his work. His journey in exploring the interconnections between various faith traditions and philosophical systems has spanned several decades, with a particular focus on the ancient wisdom of Taoism and its relevance in the modern world.

Facebook: www.facebook.com/tuffley/

Contents

Preface

Taoist leadership, or the art of subtle influence, is key to achieving harmonious goals across all levels of society. This ancient wisdom offers an alternative to aggressive, visible leadership styles. It's about influencing others to want to achieve objectives by creating an environment where desired outcomes arise naturally.

Unlike conventional leadership that prizes charismatic, highly visible leaders, Taoist leadership works behind the scenes. The ideal leader creates optimal conditions for teams to thrive while shielding them from external pressures. Teams see their achievements as their own, fostering deep ownership and motivation.

Humility is crucial in this leadership style. The Taoist leader foregoes public acclaim, allowing them to operate without hindrance or envy. They align others' desires with objectives through vision and nuanced communication, making goal pursuit a collective endeavour.

Strategic non-action, or *wu wei*, is central to this approach. It involves creating the right conditions for people to excel, then stepping back. As Sir Richard Branson suggests; provide the right people with resources and authority, then let them work without interference.

Taoist leadership recognizes that forcing issues often creates resistance and resentment. By allowing natural evolution, the leader avoids these pitfalls, creating sustainable success and harmony.

This approach challenges us to rethink notions of power and control, suggesting that true strength lies in restraint, wisdom in humility, and leadership in fostering others' greatness. It offers a path to influence that is as powerful as it is subtle, creating harmony and achieving lasting results in a world often characterized by noise and conflict.

Contents

PREFACE I
INTRODUCTION 4
THE TAO OF LEADERSHIP 7
    SUBTLE INFLUENCE 11
    THE STEADY FORCE OF ATTITUDE 15
    MAINTAINING SIMPLICITY 19
    GRAVITAS 22
    COORDINATING COLLECTIVE EFFORT 25
    GUIDE RATHER THAN RULE 27
    UNITY OF EFFORT 30
    REPLACE RIGID RULES WITH SPONTANEITY 33
    LIKE COOKING A SMALL FISH 38
    UNITING THE GROUP INTO A TEAM 42
    AVOID MACHIAVELLIAN STRATEGIES 47
    HUMILITY 49
    COMPASSION 52
    AVOID SELF-AGGRANDISEMENT 56
    AVOID AGGRESSION 60
    USE FORCE ONLY WHEN NECESSARY 63
    CULTIVATING RESTRAINT AND HUMILITY 67
    KNOWING HOW MUCH IS ENOUGH 71
    AVOIDING ESCALATION 75
    ACCEPTING BLAME 78
    PROMOTING INDEPENDENCE 81
    EPILOGUE 84
    ABOUT THE AUTHOR 86
ABOUT THE AUTHOR 89
    OTHER BOOKS BY DAVID TUFFLEY 89
    ONE LAST THING... 90

Introduction

Having a working knowledge of the art of subtle influence, or Taoist leadership, is the key to the harmonious achievement of goals at all levels, from the family, community, to organisation, state, nation all the way up to the global community. This ancient wisdom, distilled over millennia, offers a profound alternative to the often aggressive and visible leadership styles prevalent in today's world. It is the art of guiding without seeming to guide, of influencing without apparent effort.

The essence of Taoist leadership lies in its subtlety. It is knowing how to influence others to want to achieve worthy objectives, not through coercion or manipulation, but by creating an environment where desired outcomes arise naturally. We call it subtle because when it is done masterfully, people think it was all their own doing, not realizing the gentle guidance that led them there. This approach taps into the intrinsic motivations of individuals and groups, aligning their desires with the broader objectives at hand.

The Taoist perspective on leadership runs counter to conventional wisdom that often extols the virtues of the highly visible, charismatic leader that everybody knows and loves. While such leaders can indeed be effective, the Taoist approach suggests that true mastery lies in a more understated form of leadership. The ideal Taoist leader

Taoist Leadership: The Art of Subtle Influence

works behind the scenes, creating optimal conditions for teams to thrive while shielding them from external pressures. In this carefully cultivated environment, teams see their achievements as entirely their own, fostering a deep sense of ownership and motivation.

This type of leadership is so subtle that teams may be barely aware of the leader's influence. When objectives are met and credit is allocated, the team genuinely believes, "we did it ourselves". For the Taoist leader, this is the ultimate success. They have little need for external validation or applause; the quiet satisfaction of seeing others succeed and grow is reward enough.

Humility is a cornerstone of this leadership style. While the high-profile leader often derives satisfaction from public recognition and acclaim, the Taoist leader willingly foregoes such accolades. This humility serves a strategic purpose beyond mere virtue - it allows the leader to operate without hindrance, avoiding the envy of competitors or the resistance of those intent on proving a point. By staying out of the limelight, the Taoist leader can continue their work unimpeded, their influence all the more powerful for being unnoticed.

The defining aspect of the subtle leader is their ability to align the desires of others with the objectives at hand. Through a combination of forward vision and nuanced communication skills, they create a shared sense of purpose. Rather than issuing orders or making demands, they inspire others to want what the leader wants, making the pursuit of goals a collective endeavour rather than a top-down mandate.

Taoist Leadership: The Art of Subtle Influence

Strategic non-action, or *wu wei*, is a key ingredient of this leadership style. This concept, central to Taoist philosophy, suggests that the most effective action is often non-action - not passivity, but a deliberate choice to allow situations to evolve naturally rather than forcing outcomes. In leadership, this translates to creating the right conditions for people to excel and then stepping back, resisting the urge to micromanage or interfere.

As Sir Richard Branson, a modern exemplar of this approach, puts it: *get the right people, provide them with the necessary resources and authority, then stand back and let them work without interference.* This approach recognizes that excessive control often stifles creativity and initiative, while trust and autonomy foster innovation and commitment.

The wisdom of *wu wei* in leadership lies in its recognition of the natural rhythms and dynamics of groups and situations. Forcing issues often creates resistance and resentment, undermining long-term success. By allowing people and situations to evolve naturally, the Taoist leader avoids these pitfalls, creating sustainable success and harmony.

In essence, Taoist leadership offers a path to influence that is as powerful as it is subtle. It challenges us to rethink our notions of power and control, suggesting that true strength often lies in restraint, wisdom in humility, and leadership in the ability to foster the greatness of others. In a world often characterized by noise and conflict, this ancient wisdom offers a compelling alternative - a way to lead that creates harmony, fosters growth, and achieves lasting results.

The Tao of Leadership

The essence of leadership is to have a compelling vision of how the world could be, then to communicate the vision to create enthusiasm, motivating people to want to make it so. This profound insight encapsulates the transformative power of leadership. It recognizes that true leadership goes beyond mere management or administration; it's about painting a picture of a better future and inspiring others to help bring that future into being.

The Taoist perspective can be helpful in this regard since it cultivates a strong awareness of the natural flow of events, the patterns of Nature and their influence on human societies. This alignment with natural patterns is a cornerstone of Taoist thought. It suggests that by attuning ourselves to the rhythms and cycles of the world around us, we can gain deeper insights into the forces shaping our lives and societies. This awareness becomes a powerful tool for leadership, allowing one to negotiate complex situations with greater wisdom and foresight.

With this awareness you can extend these patterns into the future and see what is possible or likely. But the future is not set in stone. Its direction is influenced by the visionaries and their ability to make their vision a reality. This nuanced understanding of the future acknowledges both the power of natural trends and the potential for human intervention. It suggests a leadership approach that is both responsive to existing conditions and proactive in shaping what's to come.

Taoist Leadership: The Art of Subtle Influence

The text then offers a compelling illustration of this principle through the example of science fiction writers. Consider for example the visions of the future created by the early science fiction writers Jules Verne and H.G. Wells. Generations of engineers have been inspired by the works of Verne and Wells, producing all manner of technologies from submarines called Nautilus that could travel 20,000 leagues under the sea without surfacing, journeys to the moon and back, and the exploration of Mars. This example beautifully demonstrates the power of visionary thinking. These writers, through their imaginative works, exercised a form of leadership that transcended time and direct authority.

The futuristic visions of later sci-fi writers like Philip K. Dick and William Gibson have also had a profound effect on the direction of technology development. It could be said that these influential writers have exercised a subtle leadership over generations of technologists and engineers. They imagined a compelling future and communicated it to the world in a way that made people enthusiastic. This observation highlights the far-reaching impact of visionary thinking. It suggests that leadership can be exercised not just through formal positions of authority, but through the power of ideas and imagination.

The text then broadens its scope, emphasizing the universal applicability of these principles: Regardless of whether you are a manager of other people, or someone with few formal relationships, the principles discussed here describe the Taoist way of influencing people. This inclusivity is a key aspect of Taoist thought, recognizing that

Taoist Leadership: The Art of Subtle Influence

the principles of harmonious influence can be applied at all levels of society.

Lao Tzu wrote the Tao Te Ching for those in positions of power and influence, people who might create a better, more harmonious world. The Tao Te Ching is a Leadership manual that has survived the test of time. Published 2,500 years ago it is the oldest book still in print. This historical context underscores the timeless nature of these principles. The enduring relevance of the Tao Te Ching speaks to the universal and fundamental nature of its insights into leadership and human dynamics.

The text concludes with an important note on the approach taken in presenting these ideas: What follows are plain English versions of a subset of the 81 original verses of the Tao Te Ching that have bearing on the broad topic of leadership. They are expressed in general terms so they can apply to the widest range of situations. Your challenge is to understand the spirit of each verse and work out ways that you can emulate the character traits. It does not tell you how to emulate, a one-size, prescriptive approach would be doomed to failure. Each person must come to their own unique version of these leadership principles. This book tells you what but not how -- you are the best person to decide what will work best for you. This approach aligns perfectly with Taoist philosophy, which emphasizes personal insight and adaptation over rigid rules. It invites readers to engage deeply with the principles, to internalize them, and to find their own unique expressions of these timeless truths.

In essence, this introduction sets the stage for a profound exploration of leadership, grounded in ancient wisdom yet relevant to modern challenges. It promises insights that are both practical and philosophical, applicable to all who seek to influence and guide, regardless of their formal position.

Subtle Influence

According to Lao Tzu, the best kind of leader to aspire to being is one whose existence is barely known by those they lead. This profound insight challenges our conventional understanding of leadership, suggesting that true mastery lies not in visibility or acclaim, but in subtle, almost imperceptible influence. Such a leader operates like the invisible hand that guides without being seen, shaping outcomes while allowing others to feel a sense of ownership and accomplishment.

The next best is loved, the next are respected and the next are ridiculed. This hierarchy of leadership effectiveness offers a nuanced view of how different leadership styles impact an organization. While being loved or respected as a leader can certainly be beneficial, Lao Tzu suggests that these qualities, though positive, may still create a dependency or focus on the leader that can be limiting. The least effective leaders, those who are ridiculed, clearly fail to inspire or guide effectively, likely due to their inability to connect with or understand their people.

Recognizing people's deep-seated need to feel in control of how they do their work, the enlightened leader avoids coercion, instead using subtle influence such as goal setting, trust and carefully worded directives like 'here is how to become the person you most want to be'. This approach acknowledges a fundamental aspect of human psychology – the desire for autonomy and self-determination. By framing guidance in terms of personal growth and aspiration, rather than as orders or demands, the enlightened leader taps into

Taoist Leadership: The Art of Subtle Influence

intrinsic motivation, a far more powerful force than external pressure.

Such subtlety means that people adopt the leader's ideas and objectives as their own. When a person 'owns' an idea, they will work hard to make it work. This is the kind of subtle influence to aspire to. This principle speaks to the power of internalization. When individuals feel that an idea or goal originates from within themselves, their commitment to it becomes deeply personal. They are no longer working to please a boss or meet an external standard, but to fulfil their own aspirations and potential.

Subtle influence allows a person to develop autonomy from which they derive the satisfaction of one who manages their own affairs. This autonomy is not just about freedom of action, but about developing a sense of personal agency and capability. As individuals grow more confident in their ability to make decisions and solve problems, they become more engaged, innovative, and resilient. The enlightened leader understands that fostering this kind of autonomy ultimately strengthens the entire organization.

The worst thing a leader can do is be tyrannical. People feel interfered with by a coercive leader. Their need for autonomy and control over how they do their work is disregarded. This is sure to generate negative reaction. This stark warning highlights the destructive nature of authoritarian leadership. When leaders attempt to control through force or fear, they not only stifle creativity and initiative but also breed resentment and resistance.

In time, such leaders are likely to be undermined, subverted or otherwise disposed of by those they lead. This

Taoist Leadership: The Art of Subtle Influence

observation speaks to the unsustainability of tyrannical leadership. Even if such leaders achieve short-term compliance, they ultimately create an environment of mistrust and discontent that will eventually lead to their downfall. People have a natural tendency to resist oppression, whether overtly or covertly, and will find ways to reclaim their autonomy.

The enlightened leader, by contrast, creates an environment where people feel empowered and valued. They understand that their role is not to dictate every action, but to provide a framework within which others can excel. This might involve setting clear goals and expectations, but then stepping back to allow individuals and teams to determine the best way to achieve those goals.

Moreover, the enlightened leader recognizes that mistakes and failures are an inevitable part of growth and innovation. Rather than punishing errors, they create a culture where calculated risks are encouraged, and failures are seen as learning opportunities. This approach fosters a sense of psychological safety that allows people to be creative, take initiative, and push boundaries without fear of reprisal.

The concept of subtle influence also extends to how the leader handles success. When goals are achieved or problems solved, the enlightened leader allows credit to flow to the team or individuals who did the work. They understand that by shining the spotlight on others, they not only boost morale and motivation but also strengthen their own influence by demonstrating humility and generosity.

In essence, the art of subtle influence as described by Lao Tzu is about creating an environment where people can

Taoist Leadership: The Art of Subtle Influence

flourish, where they feel a sense of ownership and purpose, and where they are inspired to give their best not because they are told to, but because they want to. It's a leadership style that requires patience, self-awareness, and a deep understanding of human nature. While it may not always yield immediate results, it creates a strong, resilient, and highly motivated organization in the long run.

The Steady Force of Attitude

Leading by example is the most desirable form of leadership. This simple yet profound statement encapsulates a fundamental truth about effective leadership. It recognizes that the most powerful influence a leader can exert is not through words or directives, but through their own behaviour and demeanour. This principle aligns closely with the Taoist concept of wu wei, or effortless action, where influence is exerted not through force, but through the natural alignment of one's being with the Tao.

The enlightened leader understands that it is the steady force of their attitudes, as perceived by those around them, that exerts the greatest influence, more so than their actions or their words. This insight Looks more deeply into the nature of leadership influence. It suggests that beyond specific actions or verbal communications, it is the consistent, underlying attitude of the leader that truly shapes the organizational culture and the behaviour of others. This "steady force" creates a pervasive atmosphere that subtly guides and influences all who operate within it.

People instinctively know that actions speak louder than words. If there is a difference between what a person says and what they do, it is their actions that speak the truth. This observation taps into a deep human intuition about authenticity and integrity. It highlights the importance of congruence between a leader's words and actions, acknowledging that people are highly attuned to discrepancies between the two. When such discrepancies exist, trust erodes, and the leader's influence diminishes.

Taoist Leadership: The Art of Subtle Influence

Through example, people come to know what a leader respects and values. These values become the motivating force behind people's actions. This principle underscores the power of embodied values. Rather than merely stating organizational values, the enlightened leader lives them, making them tangible and real for others to observe and emulate. This lived example becomes a far more potent motivator than any mission statement or corporate policy.

The enlightened leader therefore models high regard for honesty, flexibility and spontaneity. These specific qualities – honesty, flexibility, and spontaneity – are highlighted as particularly valuable. Honesty builds trust, the foundation of all effective relationships. Flexibility allows for adaptation and growth in a changing environment. Spontaneity encourages creativity and authenticity, countering the rigidity that can stifle an organization.

The enlightened leader avoids championing high achievers. They know that by creating a winner, they simultaneously create multiple losers who then feel undervalued. This counterintuitive approach challenges common practices in many organizations. It recognizes that while individual recognition can be motivating for the recipient, it can have unintended negative consequences for the broader team dynamic.

High achievers should be quietly congratulated and rewarded, not paraded in such a way as to make non-winners feel bad. This nuanced approach to recognition balances the need to acknowledge excellence with the importance of maintaining team cohesion and motivation. It suggests a more private, personalized approach to rewards and recognition.

Singling high achievers out for public praise creates what Stephen Covey (in 7 Habits of Highly Effective People) calls a 'scarcity mentality' in which praise is a scarce commodity that is reserved for the favoured few. This reference to Covey's work provides a theoretical framework for understanding the psychological impact of public recognition practices. The concept of 'scarcity mentality' illuminates how certain leadership behaviours can inadvertently create a competitive, zero-sum atmosphere within a team.

Talented but undervalued people tend to leave which then weakens the team. This observation highlights the practical consequences of an overly competitive or inequitable recognition system. It points to the importance of creating an environment where all team members feel valued and have opportunities for growth and recognition.

The enlightened leader brings stability to the group through the steady force of their inclusive attitudes. This statement encapsulates the overarching impact of the leader's attitude. By maintaining a consistently inclusive approach, the leader creates a stable, supportive environment that allows all team members to thrive.

They do not micro-manage. They allow people to get on with things without interference. This principle of non-interference aligns closely with Taoist philosophy. It recognizes that excessive control often stifles creativity, initiative, and personal growth. By stepping back and

Taoist Leadership: The Art of Subtle Influence

trusting their team, the enlightened leader creates space for others to develop and excel.

A related point is integrity. An enlightened leader has the integrity to be consistent with what they say and what they do. This final point brings the discussion full circle, reinforcing the critical importance of congruence between words and actions. Integrity is presented not just as a moral virtue, but as a practical necessity for effective leadership.

People generally are quick to spot hypocrisy between the two, and most know that when there is a disparity, it is what a person does that expresses the truth. This closing observation serves as a warning and a reminder. It acknowledges the perceptiveness of those being led and the potential damage that can be done by inconsistency between words and actions.

In essence, this passage paints a picture of leadership that is subtle yet profoundly influential. It emphasizes the power of consistent, embodied values and attitudes over overt directives or sporadic actions. The enlightened leader, according to this view, shapes their organization not through force or manipulation, but through the steady, pervasive influence of their own example and attitude. This approach creates a stable, inclusive environment where all members can flourish, driven by intrinsic motivation rather than external rewards or punishments.

Maintaining Simplicity

The Taoist approach to leadership emphasizes the power of simplicity and intuition over complex, socially defined protocols. Simple, intuitively derived ways of behaving that are in harmony with the Tao are generally preferable to rigid social conventions. These natural, spontaneous modes of conduct allow for greater flexibility and authentic expression.

Conversely, elaborate social protocols often create more problems than they solve. It is all too easy to make missteps or inadvertently cause offense when trying to negotiate intricate rules of etiquette or organizational procedures. Moreover, such protocols tend to create divisive in-groups and out-groups - those who know the "correct" way to behave versus those who do not. This artificial separation plays into the ego's tendency to categorize the world into "us versus them" mentalities, reinforcing tribalism and a lack of unity.

The enlightened leader recognizes that simple, intuitive leadership is inherently more inclusive and compassionate. Rather than focusing on differences or creating separation, it seeks to find common ground and shared humanity among all people. This approach fosters connection, understanding, and collaboration across diverse groups.

Modes of social behaviour that are overtly praiseworthy or designed to garner public accolades should be approached with caution. The enlightened leader is wary of virtue signalling or engaging in philanthropy primarily for show or social recognition. Such self-seeking behaviours are often rooted in a desire for external validation and esteem-boosting rather than genuine altruism.

True wisdom comes from being in tune with one's inner guidance and intuition, not from seeking the approval of others or conforming to societal expectations of what constitutes virtuous conduct. The Taoist leader practices humility and often engages in anonymous acts of kindness or philanthropy. This allows them to cultivate authentic self-esteem and act from a place of integrity, without becoming dependent on external praise or recognition.

By acting with simplicity and staying attuned to their instincts, the enlightened leader cultivates greater agility and appropriateness in their responses to emerging situations. They are not bound by precedent or rigid protocols but can fluidly adapt their approach as circumstances require. This simplicity and spontaneity endow the leader with a certain power - a clarity of purpose and action that others intuitively recognize and respect.

People naturally perceive the enlightened leader's alignment with the Tao, the underlying flow and harmony of the universe. This confers upon them that elusive quality of gravitas - a weightiness and depth of character that inspires trust and confidence in others.

To maintain this simplicity, the wise leader consciously releases themselves from the constraints of orthodoxy and tradition. While respecting the wisdom of the past, they do not allow themselves to become overly bound by it. Orthodoxy can become a mental straitjacket, stifling creativity, and limiting one's ability to respond dynamically to new challenges.

Taoist Leadership: The Art of Subtle Influence

A leader who is overly attached to tradition or precedent will tend to seek solutions in the past rather than seeing each situation with fresh eyes. They may ask, *"What did our predecessors do in this situation?"* or *"How did our esteemed leader of 1793 handle a similar crisis?"* While historical knowledge can provide valuable context, relying too heavily on prefabricated responses from the past often leads to solutions that lack true insight or relevance to present circumstances.

The enlightened leader, therefore, cultivates the ability to see each situation anew, with beginner's mind. They remain open to innovative approaches and are willing to break with tradition when necessary. By maintaining simplicity and spontaneity in their leadership style, they create an environment that encourages creativity, adaptability, and harmonious collaboration among all members of their organization or community.

Gravitas

Gravitas becomes manifest in the enlightened leader as they become more closely aligned with the Tao (which may be understood as the larger forces of Nature that flows through daily life). Such alignment naturally deepens and transforms their personality. This explanation ties the concept of gravitas to the fundamental Taoist principle of alignment with the Tao. It suggests that true gravitas is not about superficial charisma or forceful personality, but about a deep connection to the underlying principles that govern the universe. This alignment is seen as transformative, affecting the very essence of the leader's being.

The transformation is illustrated by the old saying, originally attributed to the poet Rumi, that *when a person becomes enlightened and feels themselves to be connected to everything around them, they are no longer like a drop in the ocean, but the whole ocean in a drop.* No longer an individual, but the embodiment of all there is. The cultivation of gravitas is a consequence of this transformation. This poetic metaphor beautifully captures the essence of the transformation that leads to true gravitas. It speaks to a profound shift in perspective and identity, where the leader moves beyond a limited, ego-centric view to a more expansive, interconnected understanding of reality. This shift is seen as the source of genuine gravitas.

The enlightened leader knows that treating everyone with simple dignity endows their actions with subtle but powerful influence which is an underlying quality of gravitas. This principle emphasizes the power of basic human respect. It

Taoist Leadership: The Art of Subtle Influence

suggests that true gravitas is not about projecting superiority or authority, but about recognizing and honouring the inherent dignity of all individuals. This approach creates a subtle yet profound influence that permeates all interactions.

Author John Steinbeck demonstrated leadership with his Nobel Prize winning novel *The Grapes of Wrath* (1939). In contrast, French Queen Marie-Antoinette from her privileged position showed contemptuous disregard for the welfare of the people with her *let them eat cake* comment. Though probably a journalistic cliché it sums up the attitude of the French aristocracy that so enraged the people and led to the French Revolution in 1789. These historical examples vividly illustrate the difference between leadership with gravitas and leadership without it. Steinbeck's work, which gave voice to the struggles of the marginalized, demonstrates how art and literature can embody leadership and gravitas. Marie-Antoinette's (likely apocryphal) comment, on the other hand, exemplifies the lack of gravitas that comes from disconnection and disregard for others.

More recently it has been observed that the character of a nation, or organisation or individual can be assessed by how they treat the weakest member of their group. How a person treats those over whom they have power. Do they treat them with consideration and respect, or are they harsh because they can be? Do they 'kiss up and kick down' in the social hierarchy, or do they have sameness of bearing with everyone from the highest to the lowest? This observation extends the principle of dignity and respect to a broader context. It suggests that true gravitas is revealed not in how one treats equals or superiors, but in how one treats those with less power. The phrase "*kiss up and kick down*" vividly describes the antithesis of gravitas – a duplicitous approach that lacks integrity and undermines true leadership.

Enlightened leaders do not use their position to grant themselves special rewards not available to everyone, for example executive bonuses that are many times the annual salary of ordinary employees. This principle addresses the practical application of gravitas in organizational leadership. It suggests that true gravitas is incompatible with self-serving behaviour or excessive privilege. Instead, it implies that leaders with genuine gravitas seek to create a sense of fairness and shared purpose within their organizations.

The gravitas of the servant leader is most conducive to achieving their objectives. This concluding statement ties the concept of gravitas to the idea of servant leadership. It suggests that the most effective form of gravitas comes not from asserting one's authority or status, but from a genuine commitment to serving others and the larger purpose of the organization or community.

In essence, this passage presents gravitas as a profound quality that arises from a deep alignment with universal principles, a sense of interconnectedness, and a commitment to treating all individuals with dignity and respect. It challenges conventional notions of leadership based on authority or charisma, instead presenting a model of leadership that is grounded in wisdom, empathy, and service. The leader with true gravitas, according to this view, is one who has transcended ego-driven motivations and operates from a place of deep understanding and connection with both the Tao and with all those they lead.

Taoist Leadership: The Art of Subtle Influence

Coordinating Collective Effort

Enlightened leaders possess the remarkable ability to unify diverse talents into a harmonious and coordinated effort. They understand that the whole can be greater than the sum of its parts when individual strengths are skilfully combined. These leaders create a fertile and productive environment in which winning ideas can emerge serendipitously. They recognize that such innovative concepts are often elusive and cannot be summoned on demand like a genie. Instead, they focus on cultivating the right conditions for creativity and collaboration to flourish spontaneously.

The leader can be likened to a serene mountain lake that collects water from tributaries. Just as the lake provides a calm and nurturing environment for aquatic life, the leader creates an atmosphere in which people can work productively and thrive. They have a keen eye for talent and carefully select the right individuals for each role. Once assembled, the leader ensures these team members have access to all necessary resources, whether tangible assets like equipment and funding, or intangible ones like information and support networks. Crucially, the leader also grants them the authority to make decisions within their realm of expertise.

Having set the stage for success, the enlightened leader then steps back, allowing the team the freedom to operate autonomously. This approach fosters a sense of ownership and engagement among team members. They become so deeply engrossed in their work - finding purpose, challenge, and fulfilment in their tasks - that they may almost forget

Taoist Leadership: The Art of Subtle Influence

about the leader's presence. This is not a sign of the leader's irrelevance, but rather a testament to their skill in creating a self-sustaining ecosystem of productivity.

In certain contexts, effective leadership can take on a more visible and hands-on role, akin to the conductor of an orchestra. Here, the leader's role in coordinating collective effort becomes more apparent and dynamic. The conductor doesn't play an instrument themselves, yet their contribution is vital. Through subtle gestures and expressions, they guide the timing, volume, and emotional intensity of each section of the orchestra. Without this fine-tuned coordination, the output would be discordant - a cacophony rather than a symphony. The conductor's expertise lies in bringing out the best in each musician and weaving their individual contributions into a cohesive and moving performance.

Whether operating behind the scenes or in a more prominent role, the essence of leadership remains the same: to create an environment where collective talent can shine, to provide direction without stifling individual creativity, and to coordinate efforts towards a shared goal. The true art of leadership lies in making this complex process appear effortless and natural.

Taoist Leadership: The Art of Subtle Influence

Guide Rather Than Rule

It is a well-established principle of human psychology that people inherently resist being forced into action. This resistance is not merely a quirk of human nature, but a fundamental aspect of our desire for autonomy and self-determination. When excessive force is applied in one direction, it often triggers an equal and opposite reaction, as described by Newton's third law of motion. This principle extends beyond physics into the realm of human behaviour and social dynamics.

People have a deep-seated appreciation for the ability to make their own choices. This desire for agency is a powerful motivator and can significantly impact productivity, morale, and overall satisfaction. Recognizing this, enlightened leaders, even when vested with the authority to issue direct orders, consciously choose a different approach. They understand that wielding power through commands, while sometimes necessary in emergencies, is generally less effective in fostering long-term commitment and enthusiasm.

Instead, these wise leaders opt for a more nuanced strategy of subtle influence. They guide people towards a desired course of action by providing compelling reasons to embrace it willingly. This approach aligns with the famous observation made by Dwight D. Eisenhower, the 34th President of the United States and former Supreme Commander of the Allied Expeditionary Force in Europe during World War II. Eisenhower astutely noted that *"leadership is the art of getting people to do what you want them to do because they want to do it."*

The enlightened leader achieves this delicate balance by presenting situations and options in a way that clearly demonstrates how the proposed course of action serves the individual's best interests. They take the time to explain the context, potential benefits, and broader implications of decisions. Moreover, they appeal to people's sense of purpose by illustrating how the action contributes to the greater interests of the team, organization, or community they serve.

This method of leadership requires patience, empathy, and excellent communication skills. It involves active listening to understand the perspectives and motivations of team members. By doing so, leaders can tailor their approach to resonate with each individual's values and aspirations. They create an environment where people feel heard, respected, and valued for their contributions.

Furthermore, this guiding approach fosters a culture of trust and mutual respect. When people feel that their leader considers their wellbeing and respects their autonomy, they are more likely to reciprocate with loyalty, creativity, and discretionary effort. This creates a positive feedback loop, enhancing team cohesion and organizational effectiveness.

It's important to note that guiding rather than ruling doesn't mean abdicating responsibility or avoiding difficult decisions. Leaders must still provide clear direction and make tough calls when necessary. The key difference lies in how these decisions are communicated and implemented. By involving team members in the decision-making process where possible and explaining the rationale behind choices, leaders can maintain their authority while preserving the team's sense of agency.

The philosophy of guiding rather than ruling recognizes that sustainable, high-performance leadership is built on influence, not coercion. It's about creating an environment where people are inspired to give their best, not because they're ordered to, but because they genuinely want to contribute to a shared vision of success.

Taoist Leadership: The Art of Subtle Influence

Unity of Effort

Unity of effort is a cornerstone of effective leadership and organizational success. It is achieved when an enlightened leader successfully creates a shared vision that resonates deeply with their team, inspiring genuine enthusiasm, and commitment. This shared vision acts as a powerful unifying force, aligning diverse talents and perspectives towards a common goal.

The process begins with the leader's ability to articulate their vision in a compelling and inclusive manner. They paint a vivid picture of the future that excites and motivates team members, helping them see how their individual contributions fit into the larger picture. This approach taps into people's intrinsic motivation, fostering a sense of purpose that goes beyond mere compliance or the pursuit of external rewards.

Once this foundation of shared purpose is established, the enlightened leader focuses on creating the optimal conditions for success. They demonstrate a keen understanding of each team member's strengths and potential, carefully matching individuals to roles where they can thrive and make the most significant impact. This thoughtful placement not only maximizes efficiency but also enhances job satisfaction and personal growth.

Providing adequate resources is another crucial aspect of fostering unity of effort. The leader ensures that team members have access to the tools, information, and support necessary to perform their tasks effectively. This might

Taoist Leadership: The Art of Subtle Influence

include tangible resources like equipment and funding, as well as intangible assets such as training opportunities and mentorship.

Equally important is the leader's willingness to delegate authority. By empowering team members to make decisions within their areas of responsibility, the leader demonstrates trust and respect for their capabilities. This autonomy not only speeds up decision-making processes but also cultivates a sense of ownership and accountability among team members.

Once these elements are in place, the enlightened leader takes a step back, resisting the urge to micromanage. They understand that excessive oversight can stifle creativity, erode trust, and undermine the very unity of effort they seek to create. Instead, they maintain an open-door policy, providing guidance and support when needed, but allowing team members the space to apply their expertise and solve problems independently.

This approach to leadership aligns closely with the philosophy of Lao Tzu, the ancient Chinese philosopher and author of the *Tao te Ching*. Lao Tzu believed in the inherent goodness of human nature, positing that people naturally tend towards harmony and cooperation. According to this view, aggressive or unruly behaviour is not innate but rather a reaction to perceived injustice or the application of unreasonable force.

Embracing this perspective, the enlightened leader strives to create a collaborative environment founded on principles of fairness and mutual respect. They lead by example, demonstrating simplicity and modesty in their own behaviour. This approach helps to build trust and fosters a culture where team members feel valued and heard.

An important aspect of maintaining unity of effort is the leader's conscious decision to avoid creating unnecessary internal competition. While healthy competition can sometimes drive innovation and performance, the enlightened leader recognizes that excessive rivalry within a team can be counterproductive. It can lead to a focus on individual gain at the expense of collective success, undermining the collaborative spirit essential for true unity of effort.

Instead, the leader encourages a culture of cooperation and shared success. They design reward systems that recognize both individual contributions and team achievements, reinforcing the idea that the team's success is interdependent. They facilitate open communication and knowledge sharing, creating opportunities for team members to learn from each other and celebrate collective wins.

By fostering this environment of trust, respect, and shared purpose, the enlightened leader creates a powerful synergy within the team. Team members become invested not only in their individual tasks but in the overall success of the project or organization. This unity of effort often leads to increased creativity, resilience in the face of challenges, and the ability to produce more than the sum of individual contributions.

Unity of effort is both the goal and the result of enlightened leadership. It emerges from a careful balance of vision, trust, empowerment, and collaborative culture, creating an environment where people naturally want to work together towards shared objectives.

Replace Rigid Rules with Spontaneity

In many organizations, there exists a pervasive culture of rigid rules and strict conformity. These systems operate under the misguided belief that tightly controlled environments lead to predictable, efficient outcomes. However, this approach often ignores a fundamental aspect of human nature: our inherent resistance to unreasonable force and our desire for autonomy.

When faced with an inflexible set of rules that leave no room for individual judgment or creativity, people's natural reaction is often one of frustration and anger. This emotional response isn't merely a matter of preference; it's deeply rooted in our psychological makeup. Humans have an innate need for self-determination and the ability to exercise their own decision-making faculties.

The consequences of such rigid systems can be far-reaching and detrimental to the organization. Resentment begins to build among employees, who feel undervalued and constrained. This resentment doesn't simply dissipate; instead, it often manifests in subtle (and sometimes not-so-subtle) acts of subversion. People start looking for loopholes, ways to circumvent the rules without outright breaking them. They may engage in malicious compliance, following the letter of the rules while deliberately ignoring their spirit. In many cases, they succeed in these efforts, undermining the very system that was meant to ensure order and productivity.

Taoist Leadership: The Art of Subtle Influence

When management becomes aware of this trend, their knee-jerk reaction is often to double down on control measures. They may implement even stricter rules, increase surveillance, or impose harsher penalties for non-compliance. This reaction, while understandable from a certain perspective, typically exacerbates the problem. It creates a adversarial relationship between management and employees, further eroding trust and cooperation.

As employees feel increasingly cornered and disrespected, their reactions intensify. This can lead to more overt forms of resistance, such as decreased productivity, increased absenteeism, or even organized opposition to management policies. Thus, a negative cycle of behaviour is set in motion, with each side's actions reinforcing and amplifying the other's negative responses.

The fundamental issue with rigidly defined rules is that they represent a form of extremism in organizational management. Like all extremes, they tend to produce sharply polarized attitudes among those affected by them. On one side, you have those who strictly adhere to and enforce the rules, often becoming inflexible and losing sight of the broader objectives. On the other side are those who feel oppressed by the rules and actively resist them, sometimes to the point of sabotaging organizational goals.

These polarized attitudes are inherently counter-productive. They create an environment where collaboration becomes difficult, if not impossible. Instead of working together towards common goals, people become focused on either enforcing or evading rules. This adversarial atmosphere stifles creativity, reduces motivation, and

Taoist Leadership: The Art of Subtle Influence

ultimately hampers the organization's ability to adapt and thrive in a changing environment.

Enlightened leaders understand this dynamic and recognize the dangers of such extremes. They draw wisdom from observing how polarity operates in Nature, where balance and harmony often emerge from the interplay of opposing forces. Just as ecosystems thrive through diversity and adaptability rather than rigid uniformity, organizations can benefit from a more flexible and nuanced approach to management.

Instead of relying on strict rules and punitive measures, these leaders focus on achieving their objectives through more subtle and collaborative means. They cultivate an environment of trust and open communication, where employees feel valued and heard. This approach doesn't mean abandoning all structure or accountability; rather, it involves creating guidelines that are flexible enough to accommodate individual circumstances and encourage personal initiative.

One of the key strategies employed by enlightened leaders is to project a straightforward, down-to-earth honesty in their interactions with others. This authenticity serves multiple purposes. First, it inspires trust and confidence among team members. When people believe their leader is genuine and transparent, they're more likely to buy into the organization's vision and goals. Second, this honest approach provides a model for others to emulate, fostering a culture of integrity throughout the organization.

By replacing rigid rules with a more spontaneous and adaptable approach, enlightened leaders create space for innovation and personal growth. They understand that when people feel trusted and empowered, they're more likely to take ownership of their work and go above and beyond what any rule could mandate. This doesn't mean chaos or a lack of direction; rather, it involves setting clear expectations and goals while allowing flexibility in how those goals are achieved.

Moreover, this approach recognizes the diversity of talents and perspectives within an organization. Instead of trying to fit everyone into the same mold, it allows individuals to contribute in ways that play to their strengths. This not only leads to better outcomes but also increases job satisfaction and employee engagement.

In practice, replacing rigid rules with spontaneity might involve:

1. Focusing on outcomes rather than processes, allowing team members to find innovative solutions.
2. Encouraging open dialogue and constructive feedback at all levels of the organization.
3. Implementing flexible work arrangements that trust employees to manage their time effectively.
4. Fostering a culture of continuous learning and adaptation, where mistakes are seen as opportunities for growth rather than cause for punishment.
5. Regularly reviewing and updating guidelines to ensure they remain relevant and supportive of the organization's goals.

By embracing this more flexible and human-cantered approach, organizations can create environments where people genuinely want to contribute their best efforts. This leads to higher productivity, greater innovation, and a more resilient organization capable of thriving in the face of change and challenges.

Taoist Leadership: The Art of Subtle Influence

Like Cooking a Small Fish

The art of leading a large organization bears a striking resemblance to the delicate process of cooking a small fish. This enigmatic analogy, rooted in ancient wisdom, expresses a profound truth about effective leadership. Just as a chef must exercise restraint and finesse when preparing a delicate fish, an enlightened leader must maintain a light, nuanced touch in guiding their organization.

When cooking a small fish, excessive stirring or manipulation can cause the delicate flesh to fall apart in the pan, ruining the dish. Similarly, in organizational leadership, too much direct intervention or micromanagement can disrupt the delicate balance of teams, processes, and relationships that make up the fabric of a company. The enlightened leader understands that their role is not to control every aspect of the organization, but to create an environment where people and processes can function optimally with minimal interference.

This principle becomes particularly crucial when an organization faces challenges. In times of difficulty, there's often a temptation for leaders to take decisive, sweeping action. However, just as aggressively stirring a delicate fish can destroy its texture, too much action from a leader during turbulent times can exacerbate problems rather than solve them. Overzealous intervention can create unintended consequences, disrupt established systems, and undermine the confidence and autonomy of team members.

Taoist Leadership: The Art of Subtle Influence

Instead, the enlightened leader recognizes that not every problem requires an immediate or drastic solution. They understand that some challenges are complex and multifaceted, defying simple fixes. In such cases, the wisest course of action may be to step back and allow the situation to evolve naturally. This doesn't mean abdicating responsibility, but rather having the patience and wisdom to recognize when direct intervention might do more harm than good.

By adopting this approach, the leader acknowledges the power of natural forces within an organization. Just as ecosystems often find balance without external intervention, organizational dynamics can sometimes resolve themselves if given the space and time to do so. This might involve allowing teams to work through conflicts on their own, giving new initiatives time to gain traction, or letting market forces play out before making major strategic shifts.

Moreover, this culture of simplicity and non-interference creates an environment where dishonesty and subterfuge become more apparent. When a leader isn't constantly meddling or micromanaging, those engaging in deceptive practices often find their strategies rendered ineffective. The clarity that comes from a less cluttered organizational landscape makes it easier to spot inconsistencies or unethical behaviour.

The wise leader, therefore, treads lightly, understanding that their primary role is to set the overall direction and create the conditions for success, rather than to dictate every move. They recognize that each team member brings unique skills, perspectives, and potential to the table. By providing clear goals and necessary resources, then stepping back, they allow this potential to flourish.

Conversely, a micro-managing leader can severely inhibit the creativity and autonomy of their team. When employees feel constantly watched and second-guessed, they're less likely to take initiative, propose innovative ideas, or fully engage with their work. This not only stifles individual growth but also limits the organization's ability to adapt and thrive in a rapidly changing environment.

Implementing this "light touch" leadership style requires a high degree of self-awareness and confidence. Leaders must trust in their team's abilities and resist the urge to jump in at the first sign of difficulty. This approach might involve:

1. Setting clear expectations and goals but allowing flexibility in how they're achieved.
2. Providing resources and support, then stepping back to let teams work autonomously.
3. Encouraging open communication and feedback, creating channels for concerns to be raised without constant oversight.
4. Recognizing and celebrating successes, reinforcing the team's ability to solve problems independently.
5. Intervening only when absolutely necessary and doing so in a way that empowers rather than undermines.

By embracing this approach, leaders can create organizations that are more resilient, innovative, and adaptable. Just as a perfectly cooked fish retains its delicate texture and flavour, an organization led with a light touch maintains its agility and vitality.

Taoist Leadership: The Art of Subtle Influence

However, it's important to note that this approach doesn't mean being passive or uninvolved. Like a skilled chef who knows exactly when to flip the fish or adjust the heat, an enlightened leader must be keenly attuned to the subtle cues and rhythms of their organization. They must know when to provide guidance, when to challenge, and when to step back.

The art of leading like cooking a small fish is about finding the perfect balance between action and restraint, guidance and trust, vision and adaptability. It's a nuanced approach that requires patience, wisdom, and a deep understanding of human nature and organizational dynamics. When mastered, it allows leaders to nurture thriving, dynamic organizations that can negotiate the complexities of the modern business landscape with grace and effectiveness.

Taoist Leadership: The Art of Subtle Influence

Uniting the Group into a Team

The enlightened leader understands that the true strength of an organization lies not in the exceptional performance of a few individuals, but in the collective effort and growth of the entire group. This leader makes it their primary mission to foster an environment where every member of the organization has the opportunity for fulfilment and higher attainment.

Unlike traditional leadership models that often focus on identifying and nurturing only the top performers, the enlightened leader takes a more holistic and inclusive approach. They recognize that each individual, regardless of their current performance level, has unique potential and value to contribute to the organization. This perspective shifts the focus from mere talent management to comprehensive human development.

For the enlightened leader, the concept of "worthy of preferment" is fundamentally flawed. They understand that potential is not always immediately apparent, and that growth often occurs in unexpected ways and at varying paces. By avoiding the trap of categorizing team members into "high potentials" and "others," they create a more equitable and motivating environment for all.

This inclusive approach extends to those who might be considered lesser performers in a traditional sense. Rather than marginalizing or dismissing these individuals, the enlightened leader views them as valuable members of the group who can be supported and elevated. They recognize that current performance is not always indicative of future potential and that with the right support and opportunities, these team members can make significant strides in their development and contribution to the organization.

The leader actively seeks ways to help these individuals improve and grow. This might involve providing additional education and training opportunities, offering mentorship programs, or creating stretch assignments that allow team members to develop new skills and showcase hidden talents. By investing in the growth of all team members, the leader not only improves individual performance but also enhances the overall capability and resilience of the organization.

This approach to leadership has a transformative effect on the group dynamics. When individuals feel valued and see that their growth is prioritized regardless of their current standing, it fosters a sense of belonging and loyalty. Team members begin to see themselves as part of a cohesive unit rather than as competing individuals. This shift from a group of individuals to a united team is crucial for organizational success.

The unity that emerges from this inclusive leadership style manifests in several ways:

1. Increased collaboration: When all team members feel valued, they are more likely to share ideas, resources, and support with one another. The competitive atmosphere that often plagues organizations is replaced by a culture of mutual aid and shared success.
2. Enhanced morale: Knowing that the organization is invested in their personal growth and success boosts

the morale of all team members. This positive outlook translates into increased engagement and productivity.
3. Stronger loyalty: Team members who feel supported in their growth and development are more likely to remain committed to the organization, reducing turnover and preserving institutional knowledge.
4. Improved problem-solving: A diverse team with members at various stages of development brings a wider range of perspectives to challenges, often leading to more innovative and comprehensive solutions.
5. Greater adaptability: As all team members grow and expand their skills, the organization as a whole becomes more versatile and better equipped to handle changing circumstances.

The enlightened leader's approach also fosters a strong desire to collaborate among team members. When individuals see that their colleagues' success is celebrated and supported rather than viewed as a threat, they become more willing to work together towards common goals. This collaborative spirit is reinforced by the leader's example of valuing and nurturing all team members.

Moreover, this leadership style creates a positive feedback loop. As team members witness the growth and development of their colleagues, it inspires them to pursue their own improvement. The organization becomes a learning environment where continuous growth and mutual support are the norm.

Taoist Leadership: The Art of Subtle Influence

However, implementing this inclusive approach requires patience and commitment from the leader. It may not yield immediate results in terms of performance metrics, but over time, it builds a stronger, more resilient, and more capable organization. The leader must be prepared to invest time and resources into developing all team members, even when the returns are not immediately apparent.

In practice, this might involve:

1. Regular one-on-one meetings with all team members, not just top performers, to discuss their aspirations and development plans.
2. Creating a culture that celebrates effort and improvement, not just end results.
3. Implementing cross-training programs that allow team members to develop diverse skill sets.
4. Encouraging peer-to-peer mentoring to foster a culture of shared learning and support.
5. Recognizing and rewarding collaborative efforts as much as individual achievements.

By consistently applying these principles, the enlightened leader transforms a disparate group of individuals into a cohesive, motivated team. This team is united not just by common goals, but by a shared sense of value and a collective commitment to growth and success. In such an environment, the desire to collaborate becomes intrinsic to the team's culture, driving the organization towards greater achievements and resilience in the face of challenges.

The enlightened leader's approach to uniting the group into a team is about creating a rising tide that lifts all boats. By nurturing the potential in every team member and fostering a culture of inclusive growth, they create an organization that is more than the sum of its parts – a truly united and high-performing team.

Avoid Machiavellian Strategies

In leadership and organizational management, the temptation to use clever schemes and coercive tactics for quick results is ever-present. These Machiavellian strategies, advocating cunning and manipulation, seem appealing but are fundamentally flawed. While they might yield immediate benefits, wise leaders recognize the significant long-term costs.

Clever schemes often backfire, producing unintended consequences. Trust erodes when manipulation is discovered, breeding resentment and resistance. Leaders known for scheming damage their reputation, hindering future collaborations. Ethical compromises lead to increasingly questionable behaviour, and maintaining complex schemes becomes unsustainable.

In contrast, wise leaders embrace simple honesty. This approach, though potentially slower, offers lasting advantages. It builds trust through straightforward communication, creates sustainable relationships, and provides clarity of purpose. Honest leadership reduces stress by eliminating the need to maintain false narratives and attracts like-minded individuals, fostering meaningful collaborations.

The simplicity advocated by enlightened leaders stems from a deep understanding of human nature and organizational dynamics. It manifests in intuitive actions that resonate with people's desire for authenticity. This leadership style contrasts sharply with Machiavellian deception, which inevitably unravels in our interconnected world.

Enlightened leaders consciously avoid clever strategies and political maneuverings. They recognize that such behaviours are contagious, potentially creating a toxic culture of mistrust and internal competition. Instead, they opt for simplicity and directness, setting an example that fosters transparency, streamlines decision-making, encourages authenticity, and builds organizational resilience.

Implementing this approach demands courage and commitment. Leaders must engage in difficult conversations, make unpopular decisions, and sometimes accept slower progress for long-term integrity. They must communicate clearly about goals and challenges, be transparent in decision-making, admit mistakes, encourage open feedback, and align rewards with values of honesty.

This leadership style creates a positive ripple effect. Team members, inspired by the leader's example, adopt similar behaviours in their interactions. This alignment of values and actions strengthens the organization's culture and reputation, fostering trust and collaboration.

While Machiavellian strategies may seem tempting in high-pressure environments, enlightened leaders recognize their ultimate futility. By choosing simplicity, honesty, and directness, they create more resilient, ethical, and successful organizations. This approach not only benefits individual entities but contributes to a more transparent and trustworthy business environment overall.

Humility

The enlightened leader possesses a profound understanding of the paradoxical nature of effective leadership. They recognize that to truly elevate themselves in a leadership capacity, they must paradoxically remain grounded and humble in their actions and words. This approach is not a mere tactic or strategy, but a genuine embodiment of humility that permeates every aspect of their leadership style.

By consistently demonstrating sincere humility, the leader creates a powerful connection with their team. This humility manifests in various ways: listening more than speaking, valuing diverse perspectives, admitting mistakes, and showing genuine interest in the lives and experiences of team members at all levels. The leader avoids the trappings of ego and self-importance, instead focusing on the collective success of the organization and the growth of individuals within it.

This humble approach is perceived by others as a complete identification with the people. It breaks down the traditional barriers that often exist between leadership and the workforce, creating a sense of unity and shared purpose. Team members begin to see the leader not as a distant figure of authority, but as someone who understands and values their experiences and contributions.

The power of this approach lies in its ability to engender deep trust. People instinctively recognize that a leader who positions themselves below them in terms of attitude and behaviour is likely to have interests aligned with their own. This alignment is not superficial or manipulative; it stems from a genuine belief in the collective importance of every individual in the organization. When team members feel that their leader is working alongside them rather than above them, it creates a powerful sense of shared purpose and mutual respect.

Moreover, when a leader refrains from acting superior or projecting an air of unattainable authority, it allows people to see themselves reflected in the leader. This reflection is profoundly impactful. Team members begin to recognize their own potential for leadership and growth, seeing in their humble leader a model of what they themselves could become. This recognition often transforms into deep respect, and in many cases, even a form of love – not in a personal sense, but in the sense of profound appreciation and loyalty.

The humble leader understands that true authority comes not from titles or positions, but from the willing respect and cooperation of others. By consistently demonstrating humility, they create an environment where people are eager to follow, not out of obligation or fear, but out of genuine admiration and shared vision.

This approach to leadership requires great strength of character. It demands that the leader set aside their ego, resist the temptation to showcase their own accomplishments, and remain focused on the success and well-being of others. It requires constant self-reflection and a willingness to grow and learn from every interaction.

In practice, the humble leader might be found engaging in tasks typically reserved for junior team members, seeking

Taoist Leadership: The Art of Subtle Influence

input from all levels of the organization before making decisions, or publicly acknowledging their own mistakes and areas for improvement. They create an open-door policy that is more than just words – it's a genuine invitation for dialogue and collaboration.

The impact of this leadership style extends beyond the immediate team or organization. It sets a tone for how business can be conducted with integrity and mutual respect. It challenges the notion that leadership must be synonymous with dominance or superiority. Instead, it presents a model of leadership that is inclusive, empowering, and deeply human.

As this approach to leadership takes root, it transforms the entire organizational culture. People begin to emulate the leader's humility in their own interactions, creating a ripple effect of respect, openness, and collaboration. The organization becomes a place where ideas flow freely, where mistakes are viewed as opportunities for learning, and where every individual feels valued and heard.

Ultimately, the enlightened leader who embraces humility creates more than just a successful organization – they nurture a community of individuals united in purpose and mutual respect. This approach may not always be the fastest path to short-term gains, but it builds a foundation for sustainable success and fulfilment that extends far beyond the balance sheet. In a world often characterized by ego-driven leadership, the humble leader stands out as a beacon of wisdom and true strength, inspiring not just compliance, but genuine commitment and shared vision.

Compassion

The essence of exemplary leadership lies in the cultivation and expression of compassion, modesty, and a willingness to eschew the limelight. This profound understanding, rooted in ancient wisdom and reinforced by modern leadership studies, suggests that true influence and lasting impact stem not from ostentatious displays of power or authority, but from a deep well of empathy and humility.

Compassion, as understood by Lao Tzu and other great thinkers, is far more than mere sympathy or pity. It is an active force, a way of engaging with the world that recognizes the inherent dignity and worth of every individual. When a leader embodies compassion, it has a mysterious and deeply transformative effect not only on their own mind but also on the minds of those they encounter.

This transformative power of compassion operates on multiple levels. At its most immediate, it creates an environment of trust and openness. When people feel that their leader genuinely cares about their well-being and understands their challenges, they are more likely to engage fully, take risks, and contribute their best efforts. This compassionate approach breaks down barriers of fear and mistrust that often stifle creativity and collaboration in organizations.

Moreover, compassion has a ripple effect that extends far beyond immediate interactions. As team members experience and benefit from a compassionate leadership style, they tend to emulate this approach in their own interactions with

Taoist Leadership: The Art of Subtle Influence

colleagues, clients, and stakeholders. This creates a virtuous cycle, gradually transforming the culture of the entire organization and even influencing its broader ecosystem.

The enlightened leader who manifests compassion in their dealings with the world does so not as a strategic ploy, but as a genuine expression of their understanding of human nature and interconnectedness. They recognize that every decision, every policy, and every interaction have the potential to impact lives in profound ways. This awareness infuses their leadership with a sense of responsibility and care that goes beyond mere profit or efficiency metrics.

Modesty, another hallmark of this leadership style, complements compassion beautifully. A modest leader does not seek to dominate conversations or claim credit for every success. Instead, they create space for others to shine, recognizing and celebrating the contributions of team members at all levels. This modesty is not self-deprecation or false humility, but a genuine recognition of the collective nature of achievement and the importance of every individual's role in the larger picture.

By not thrusting themselves into the limelight, the compassionate and modest leader allows the work and the team to speak for itself. This approach builds a sense of collective ownership and pride among team members, who feel valued not just for their contributions but for their inherent worth as individuals. It also fosters an environment where innovation can flourish, as people feel safe to express ideas and take calculated risks without fear of overshadowing or displeasing an ego-driven leader.

Taoist Leadership: The Art of Subtle Influence

The lasting effect on the world that Lao Tzu attributed to compassion is manifest in various ways through this leadership style. Organizations led with compassion tend to be more resilient in the face of challenges, as team members are more willing to support each other and go above and beyond in difficult times. They also tend to be more innovative and adaptable, as the open and trusting environment encourages the free flow of ideas and constructive feedback.

Furthermore, compassionate leadership often results in more sustainable business practices. Leaders who genuinely care about the well-being of others are more likely to consider the long-term impacts of their decisions on employees, communities, and the environment. This holistic view leads to strategies that balance short-term gains with long-term sustainability and social responsibility.

In practice, the enlightened leader manifests compassion through active listening, empathetic communication, and a genuine concern for the personal and professional growth of team members. They create policies that support work-life balance, mental health, and individual development. They approach conflicts and challenges with a mindset of understanding and reconciliation rather than blame or punishment.

This compassionate approach does not mean avoiding difficult decisions or shirking responsibilities. On the contrary, it often requires great courage to lead with compassion, especially in high-pressure or competitive environments. The enlightened leader must sometimes make tough choices, but they do so with transparency, explaining

Taoist Leadership: The Art of Subtle Influence

their rationale and showing genuine concern for those affected.

By consistently manifesting compassion in their dealings with the world, the enlightened leader creates a legacy that extends far beyond their immediate sphere of influence. They inspire others to lead with empathy and understanding, contributing to a broader shift in how we conceive of leadership and success in business and society.

In a world marked by division, competition, and short-term thinking, the compassionate leader stands as a beacon of hope and a model for a more sustainable and fulfilling approach to leadership. They demonstrate that it is possible to achieve great things while also nurturing the human spirit and contributing to the greater good. This approach to leadership not only benefits organizations but has the potential to contribute to a more compassionate and harmonious society as a whole.

Avoid Self-Aggrandisement

In leadership and personal conduct, the Taoist principle of avoiding self-aggrandizement holds profound wisdom. This principle recognizes a fundamental truth about human social dynamics: there exists a natural levelling mechanism in group psychology that seeks to balance the excesses of those who promote themselves too forcefully or boastfully. This mechanism serves as a counterweight to individuals who, through their self-aggrandizing behaviour, create instability in the social fabric.

The wise leader, understanding this principle, cultivates a demeanour of modesty and restraint. They recognize that being overly visible or boastful about one's achievements often leads to negative consequences. This is not to say that genuine accomplishments should be hidden or downplayed, but rather that they should be presented with humility and in proper context. The enlightened person understands that excessive self-promotion often backfires, triggering resistance and resentment from others.

This levelling mechanism in group psychology operates as a form of social homeostasis. When an individual or entity becomes too dominant or self-aggrandizing, it creates an imbalance that the group instinctively seeks to correct. This correction can manifest in various ways, from subtle social ostracism to more overt challenges to the individual's authority or reputation. By avoiding excessive self-promotion, the wise leader pre-empts these negative reactions and maintains a more harmonious relationship with their peers and subordinates.

Taoist Leadership: The Art of Subtle Influence

Moreover, self-aggrandizement often creates a state of excess, which in Taoist thought is seen as inherently unstable and unsustainable. Excess, whether in self-promotion or any other aspect of life, indicates that a peak has been reached and decline is imminent. The enlightened person recognizes this pattern and discretely removes themselves from the situation before the inevitable backlash occurs. They understand that even the most popular or successful individuals will face criticism and challenges, regardless of how diligently they work to maintain their position.

Closely related to the avoidance of self-aggrandizement is the principle of avoiding hypocrisy. The wise leader understands that hypocrisy is particularly toxic to their credibility and effectiveness. They strive not only to avoid being hypocritical but also to avoid even the appearance of hypocrisy. This requires a high degree of self-awareness and consistency in one's words and actions.

One common form of hypocrisy that the enlightened person carefully avoids is the temptation to agree with different people in private discussions while expressing contradictory opinions to others. While this approach might seem politically expedient in the short term, allowing one to curry favor with various factions, it ultimately undermines trust and respect. The wise leader knows that maintaining the integrity of their position, even if it means occasionally disagreeing with others, is crucial for long-term success and credibility.

This commitment to consistency and integrity may not always be popular. Indeed, the person of integrity often finds themselves in the challenging position of pleasing no one, particularly in situations of conflict or competing interests. By refusing to take sides or tell people simply what they want to hear, the leader of integrity may face criticism from all quarters. However, this steadfast adherence to principle ultimately earns them a reputation for fairness, impartiality, and trustworthiness that is far more valuable than any short-term gains achieved through duplicity.

The enlightened person understands that any benefits gained through hypocrisy or inconsistency are inherently short-lived. Relationships built on false pretenses or manipulative agreement are fragile and prone to collapse. The friend won through insincere agreement today may well become an enemy tomorrow when the truth of one's actual position becomes clear. In contrast, relationships built on honest, consistent interaction, even when there is disagreement, tend to be more robust and enduring.

Ultimately, the avoidance of self-aggrandizement and hypocrisy is rooted in a deeper understanding of human nature and social dynamics. The wise leader recognizes that true influence and respect are not gained through self-promotion or manipulation, but through consistent, principled action and genuine concern for others. They achieve simplicity in their leadership through spontaneous, intuitive actions based on this understanding of human nature and the specific situation at hand.

This approach stands in stark contrast to Machiavellian strategies that prioritize short-term gains through manipulation and deceit. While such tactics might yield immediate results, they invariably lead to long-term failure as they erode trust and create a climate of suspicion and

Taoist Leadership: The Art of Subtle Influence

resentment. The Taoist approach, focusing on integrity, consistency, and humble effectiveness, may be less flashy but ultimately proves more sustainable and fulfilling.

By adopting these principles, the enlightened leader cultivates a leadership style characterized by quiet competence, unwavering integrity, and genuine concern for the well-being of others. This approach not only leads to more stable and harmonious social dynamics but also allows the leader to navigate the complexities of human relationships with grace and wisdom. By avoiding the pitfalls of self-aggrandizement and hypocrisy, they create a foundation for lasting success and positive influence, embodying the Taoist ideal of effortless action in harmony with natural principles.

Avoid Aggression

In the Taoist approach to leadership, aggression in all its forms is viewed as counterproductive and should be consciously avoided. Aggression, whether physical, verbal, or psychological, creates an imbalance - an excess of force that inevitably triggers counter-reactions. This principle applies not only to interpersonal dynamics but also to organizational strategies and societal interactions.

The wise leader understands that where decisive action is necessary, it should be carried out assertively rather than aggressively. Assertion and aggression, while sometimes confused, are fundamentally different approaches. Assertion is a form of restrained action that respects the rights and dignity of all parties involved, including oneself. It is characterized by clear communication, firm boundaries, and a commitment to fairness. Aggression, on the other hand, occurs when an individual or group prioritizes their own rights and desires over those of others, often leading to conflict and resentment.

In practice, assertive leadership involves stating one's needs and expectations clearly while remaining open to dialogue and compromise. It means standing firm on important principles without resorting to intimidation or coercion. Aggressive leadership, in contrast, often relies on fear, dominance, and the suppression of opposing viewpoints.

The enlightened person recognizes that aggression, in all its manifestations, is a form of excess. In the natural world,

Taoist Leadership: The Art of Subtle Influence

excess invariably produces a neutralizing reaction - a return to balance. The same principle applies in human affairs. Aggressive actions or policies may yield short-term gains, but they almost always provoke resistance and backlash, ultimately undermining the aggressor's goals.

Moreover, aggression is inherently wasteful. In individuals and groups, aggressive behaviour consumes vast amounts of energy and resources, leading to depletion and weakening over time. This depletion occurs not only on a physical level but also emotionally and spiritually. Aggressive individuals often find themselves isolated and exhausted, while aggressive organizations may face high turnover, low morale, and a hostile external environment.

In contrast, restrained action - the hallmark of assertive behaviour - uses energy economically and constructively in pursuit of goals. By avoiding unnecessary conflict and focusing on clear communication and mutual respect, assertive leaders conserve their own resources while also preserving the wellbeing of those around them. This approach allows for more sustainable, long-term success.

The wise leader understands that true success does not have to come at the expense of others. Instead, they actively seek out win-win scenarios where all parties can benefit. This approach is not only more ethical but often more effective in achieving lasting results. By considering the needs and perspectives of all stakeholders, leaders can often uncover innovative solutions that create value for everyone involved.

This win-win philosophy is deeply in keeping with the Tao, the fundamental principle of harmony and balance in the universe. Just as natural ecosystems thrive through complex webs of mutually beneficial relationships, human systems function best when they prioritize cooperation over competition, and mutual benefit over one-sided advantage.

In practical terms, avoiding aggression and embracing assertive, win-win approaches can manifest in various ways:

1. In negotiations, seeking to understand the other party's interests and finding creative ways to meet both sides' needs.
2. In conflict resolution, focusing on the issue at hand rather than attacking individuals or groups.
3. In organizational culture, fostering an environment of open communication, mutual respect, and collaborative problem-solving.
4. In strategic planning, considering the long-term impacts of decisions on all stakeholders, not just short-term gains for a select few.

By consistently choosing assertion over aggression and seeking mutually beneficial outcomes, the enlightened leader creates a ripple effect of positive change. This approach not only leads to more sustainable success but also contributes to a more harmonious and balanced world, in alignment with the deepest principles of Taoist wisdom.

Use Force Only When Necessary

In the Taoist approach to leadership, the use of force is viewed as a last resort, to be employed only when all other options have been exhausted. The wise leader understands that force, whether physical, economic, or psychological, is a powerful tool that should be wielded with great caution and restraint. When circumstances truly make it unavoidable, the rare use of force may be sanctioned, but it is never undertaken lightly or without careful consideration of the consequences.

When force must be used, the enlightened leader approaches it with a heavy heart and a clear sense of responsibility. They express genuine regret at having to resort to such measures, making it evident to all involved that the use of force brings them no satisfaction or pleasure. This attitude of reluctance and solemn duty helps to mitigate the potential negative consequences of forceful action, both in terms of practical outcomes and in maintaining the leader's moral authority.

The wise leader's approach to force mirrors the patterns observed in Nature. In the natural world, instances of overwhelming force are relatively rare and typically occur only in response to extreme circumstances. Much like how a peaceful forest might occasionally be rocked by a powerful storm or how a dormant volcano might erupt after centuries of quiescence, these events are the exception rather than the rule.

Taoist Leadership: The Art of Subtle Influence

Most of the time, Nature operates through subtle, gradual processes that bring about slow, evolutionary change in the environment. The gentle persistence of flowing water shapes landscapes over millennia. The patient work of microorganisms enriches soil over generations. The slow dance of tectonic plates reshapes continents across eons. These processes, while less dramatic than sudden bursts of force, are ultimately more transformative and sustainable.

The wise leader emulates this natural pattern in their leadership style. They understand that lasting change and true progress are most often achieved through patient, persistent effort rather than through sudden, forceful interventions. This approach manifests in various ways:

1. In decision-making, favouring thoughtful deliberation and consensus-building over unilateral declarations.
2. In problem-solving, preferring to address root causes through systemic changes rather than treating symptoms with quick fixes.
3. In conflict resolution, prioritizing dialogue, negotiation, and mediation over coercion or punitive measures.
4. In implementing changes, opting for gradual transitions that allow for adaptation rather than abrupt shifts that may provoke resistance.

By adopting this nature-inspired approach, the enlightened leader can negotiate complex situations with grace and effectiveness. They understand that force, while sometimes necessary, often creates unintended consequences and can damage the delicate web of relationships that underlies any successful organization or society.

Taoist Leadership: The Art of Subtle Influence

Moreover, the wise leader recognizes that the frequent use of force often indicates a failure of leadership rather than its success. If a leader must constantly resort to forceful measures to achieve their goals, it suggests a lack of vision, persuasive ability, or the trust and cooperation of those they lead.

Instead, the Taoist leader cultivates an environment where force is rarely needed. They do this by:

1. Building strong, trusting relationships with all stakeholders.
2. Fostering a culture of open communication and mutual respect.
3. Anticipating potential conflicts and addressing them proactively before they escalate.
4. Leading by example, demonstrating the values and behaviours they wish to see in others.

In this way, the need for force becomes increasingly rare, as the organization or community naturally aligns itself with the leader's vision through shared understanding and common purpose.

When force must be used, the wise leader ensures that it is proportional to the situation, precisely targeted, and limited in duration. They remain mindful of the potential for escalation and seek to de-escalate as soon as possible, returning to more harmonious modes of interaction.

By reserving force for truly exceptional circumstances and focusing instead on gradual, collaborative approaches to change, the enlightened leader creates a more stable, resilient, and harmonious environment. This approach not only leads to more sustainable outcomes but also aligns with the fundamental Taoist principle of working in harmony with the natural flow of events rather than against it.

Taoist Leadership: The Art of Subtle Influence

Cultivating Restraint and Humility

In the realm of organizational leadership, the Taoist principle of cultivating restraint and humility takes on particular significance, especially for powerful and successful entities. Powerful organizations, whether they be corporations, governments, or other institutions, often find themselves in a paradoxical position. Their abundance of resources, influence, and achievements provide them with great advantages, but simultaneously expose them to unique risks and challenges.

The wealth and influence amassed by successful organizations frequently become objects of envy and desire for others. Competitors, both internal and external, may covet these assets and seek to appropriate them for themselves. This reality can engender a sense of constant threat, leading powerful organizations to become increasingly risk-averse and even paranoid. The very drive and creativity that fuelled their initial rise to prominence can calcify into a rigid conservatism, as the fear of losing what they have gained begins to overshadow the ambition that propelled their growth.

Paradoxically, while this fear can breed excessive caution in some areas, it often coexists with a dangerous sense of invulnerability. The organization's power and past successes can foster a belief that they are unassailable, leading to a perilous complacency. This dual mindset - paranoid yet overconfident - creates a volatile foundation that can undermine the organization's long-term stability and success.

Taoist Leadership: The Art of Subtle Influence

To negotiate these treacherous waters, the wise leader understands the critical importance of cultivating modesty and restraint within the organizational culture. This approach serves as a powerful antidote to the twin dangers of paranoia and complacency, reducing the organization's vulnerability to decline through excess, entitlement, and loss of adaptability.

Modesty in this context doesn't mean downplaying genuine achievements or capabilities. Rather, it involves maintaining a realistic and balanced perspective on the organization's position. It means acknowledging strengths without becoming arrogant and recognizing weaknesses without becoming despondent. This balanced view helps the organization remain agile and responsive to changing circumstances.

Restraint, meanwhile, involves the judicious use of power and resources. It means resisting the temptation to flaunt wealth or influence unnecessarily, understanding that such displays often create more problems than they solve. Restraint also extends to decision-making processes, encouraging thoughtful consideration rather than impulsive actions based on a sense of invulnerability.

By cultivating these qualities, organizations can reap several benefits. When an organization practices modesty and restraint, it's less likely to attract undue attention or provoke hostile reactions from competitors or regulators. Advantages possessed by the organization are kept discreet, exciting neither envy nor alarm in the external world. A modest outlook helps the organization remain open to new ideas and approaches, rather than becoming overly wedded

Taoist Leadership: The Art of Subtle Influence

to past successes. This openness is crucial for continued innovation and growth.

Restraint in decision-making can lead to more thorough evaluation of risks and opportunities, helping the organization avoid pitfalls that overconfident entities might blunder into. A humble approach often fosters better relationships with employees, customers, partners, and other stakeholders. People are generally more willing to cooperate with and support organizations that don't project an air of arrogance or entitlement. By avoiding the extremes of paranoia and complacency, organizations can pursue a more balanced and sustainable path of growth and development.

Implementing this approach requires conscious effort and leadership from the top. Some strategies for cultivating restraint and humility might include regular self-assessment practices that honestly evaluate the organization's strengths and weaknesses. Encouraging a culture of constructive dissent, where challenges to prevailing wisdom are welcomed rather than suppressed, is also crucial. Organizations should emphasize long-term sustainability over short-term gains or displays of power, and practice transparency and accountability, both internally and externally.

Engaging in genuine corporate social responsibility efforts that create value for the broader community, not just shareholders, can help maintain a grounded perspective. Fostering a learning organization mentality, where continuous improvement and adaptation are prized over maintaining the status quo, further reinforces the principles of humility and restraint.

By embracing these principles, powerful organizations can negotiate the complex landscape of success with greater wisdom and resilience. They can maintain their strengths while avoiding the pitfalls that often accompany great power and success. In doing so, they embody the Taoist ideal of working in harmony with natural principles, achieving lasting success through balance, restraint, and humility.

Taoist Leadership: The Art of Subtle Influence

Knowing How Much is Enough

In the Taoist approach to leadership and organizational management, the concept of "knowing how much is enough" stands as a cornerstone principle. This idea directly challenges the prevalent mindset of endless growth and accumulation that dominates much of modern business and personal philosophy. At its core, this principle recognizes that greed is not just a minor flaw, but a serious character defect that can have far-reaching negative consequences for individuals, organizations, and society as a whole.

Greed manifests as an insatiable desire for more – more wealth, more power, more possessions – often far beyond what is needed for comfort or security. This endless wanting stems from a fundamental misunderstanding of what truly brings fulfillment and happiness. The greedy individual or organization falls into the trap of believing that acquisition and accumulation are the paths to satisfaction and success. However, this belief is fundamentally flawed.

One of the most insidious aspects of greed is its impact on personal and organizational identity. When individuals or entities define themselves primarily by their possessions or financial worth, they lose sight of more meaningful aspects of existence. Instead of focusing on character development, ethical behaviour, or positive contributions to society, the greedy become obsessed with external markers of success. This misplaced focus stunts personal growth and can lead to a hollow, unfulfilling existence, no matter how much wealth is accumulated.

Taoist Leadership: The Art of Subtle Influence

For organizations, the consequences of greed-driven leadership can be equally problematic. When acquisitiveness becomes the central concern, it often comes at the expense of other crucial aspects of organizational health. Employee well-being, ethical practices, community relationships, and long-term sustainability may all be sacrificed in the pursuit of short-term gains or market dominance. This narrow focus not only harms the organization's internal culture but can also damage its reputation and relationships with external stakeholders.

In contrast, when organizations are run with a clear understanding of "enough" – be it in terms of profit margins, market share, or resource consumption – a remarkable transformation can occur. The energy and focus that were once directed solely towards acquisition and growth can be redirected towards more constructive ends. Without the constant pressure to exceed previous financial benchmarks at any cost, organizations can turn their attention to internal development and improvement.

This shift in focus encourages the growth of positive internal qualities within the organization. Leadership may invest more in employee development, fostering a culture of learning and innovation. Ethical considerations can take centre stage, leading to more transparent and responsible business practices. The organization might place greater emphasis on work-life balance, recognizing that well-rested, satisfied employees are ultimately more productive and creative.

Moreover, when an organization is not driven by insatiable greed, its interactions with the wider world naturally take on a more benevolent aspect. Instead of viewing every interaction as a zero-sum game where the organization must win at the expense of others, leadership can seek out mutually beneficial relationships and outcomes. This might manifest as fair treatment of suppliers, honest marketing to customers, or genuine engagement with community needs.

This benevolent approach, somewhat counterintuitively, often leads to greater long-term prosperity for the organization and its stakeholders. By building a reputation for fairness and ethical behaviour, the organization can attract loyal customers, dedicated employees, and supportive community partners. This positive ecosystem creates a sustainable foundation for success that purely profit-driven entities often struggle to achieve.

Furthermore, an organization that knows "how much is enough" is inherently less likely to engage in harmful practices. The drive for ever-increasing profits often leads companies to cut corners on safety, exploit workers, or damage the environment. By contrast, an organization content with sustainable success can prioritize harm reduction and positive impact alongside reasonable profitability.

Implementing this principle of "enough" requires a fundamental shift in mindset at all levels of an organization. It starts with leadership clearly articulating values that go beyond financial metrics. Success must be redefined to encompass not just profitability, but also employee satisfaction, community impact, environmental stewardship, and ethical integrity. Regular reflection and reassessment are necessary to ensure the organization stays true to these broader definitions of success.

This approach aligns closely with the Taoist concept of *wu wei*, or effortless action. By not struggling against the natural limits of growth and consumption, by knowing when enough is truly enough, organizations can find a harmonious place within their broader ecosystem. This harmony leads to a more sustainable, fulfilling, and ultimately successful mode of operation.

In embracing the principle of "knowing how much is enough," leaders and organizations embody the deeper wisdom of the Tao. They recognize that true wealth lies not in endless accumulation, but in finding balance, cultivating inner qualities, and contributing positively to the world around them. This approach not only leads to more ethical and sustainable business practices but also fosters a deeper sense of purpose and fulfilment for all involved.

Avoiding Escalation

In any evolving social environment, there will be conflict between opposing ideas. This is an inevitable and necessary part of growth and progress. Conflict, when managed wisely, can be a crucible for innovation and positive change. However, the manner in which these conflicts are negotiated can determine whether they lead to constructive outcomes or destructive cycles.

The enlightened person knows that the ideas that eventually prevail are those whose proponents have managed to avoid counter-reactions to the idea. This insight speaks to a deep understanding of human psychology and group dynamics. When an idea is presented aggressively or forcefully, it often triggers an equally strong defensive reaction, regardless of the idea's merit. People tend to dig in their heels and resist change when they feel attacked or threatened. The enlightened person recognizes this and takes a different approach.

They do this by avoiding aggression. Instead of trying to bludgeon others into acceptance, the wise proponent of an idea seeks to create an environment where the idea can be considered on its own merits. This might involve presenting the idea as a possibility to be explored rather than a mandate to be followed. It could mean inviting others to contribute to and shape the idea, making them co-creators rather than passive recipients.

Force is met with force, and strategy with strategy. This principle, reminiscent of Newton's third law of motion, applies as much to social interactions as it does to physics. When one party escalates a conflict through force or manipulation, the other party is likely to respond in kind. This leads to an arms race of sorts, where the original issue often becomes lost in the escalating cycle of retaliation.

Lao Tzu thought that the side that was wise enough to feel regret at the use of force would be the side that triumphs. This profound statement turns conventional wisdom on its head. In many cultures, showing regret or remorse is seen as a sign of weakness. However, Lao Tzu recognized that the ability to feel and express regret is actually a sign of deep wisdom and strength.

The side that feels regret at the use of force is likely to be more thoughtful and measured in its actions. They are more likely to seek alternative solutions and to consider the long-term consequences of their actions. This thoughtfulness can lead to more sustainable and widely accepted solutions.

Moreover, expressing regret can have a powerful disarming effect in a conflict. It can create openings for dialogue and compromise where none seemed possible before. When one side shows vulnerability and a willingness to acknowledge mistakes, it often invites a similar response from the other side, potentially breaking the cycle of escalation.

This approach to conflict resolution and idea promotion requires a high degree of emotional intelligence and self-control. It means being able to step back from one's own ego and desire for immediate victory in service of a larger, long-term goal. It involves cultivating patience and the ability to

Taoist Leadership: The Art of Subtle Influence

see beyond the immediate conflict to the underlying needs and concerns of all parties involved.

In practice, avoiding escalation might involve techniques such as active listening, where one seeks to truly understand opposing viewpoints rather than simply waiting for an opportunity to counter them. It could mean using "I" statements to express one's own feelings and needs without attacking others. It might involve looking for common ground and shared interests as a foundation for moving forward.

Importantly, avoiding escalation does not mean avoiding conflict altogether or always backing down. Rather, it means engaging in conflict in a way that is constructive rather than destructive. It means standing firm in one's principles while remaining open to dialogue and compromise.

In today's world of polarized debates and echo chambers, Lao Tzu's wisdom on avoiding escalation is more relevant than ever. By embracing these principles, leaders and individuals can negotiate conflicts more effectively, promote ideas more successfully, and contribute to a more harmonious and productive society.

Taoist Leadership: The Art of Subtle Influence

Accepting Blame

The enlightened person in organisations takes on the qualities of water. Soft and receptive with no edge and no form, water absorbs and transforms hard structures. This metaphor of water embodies the essence of adaptability and resilience that characterizes truly effective leaders. Like water, they flow around obstacles, finding paths of least resistance, yet over time, they can shape even the most unyielding environments.

By taking responsibility, including accepting the blame for situations, the enlightened person establishes their position at the centre of the organisation. This willingness to shoulder responsibility, rather than deflect it, creates a powerful gravitational force within the organizational structure. It draws people towards them, not through authority or coercion, but through respect and trust. When a leader steps forward to accept blame, it disarms potential conflicts and sets a tone of accountability throughout the entire organization.

They extend their influence outwards in a positive way. This influence spreads organically, much like ripples on a pond. It doesn't force its way through the organization but permeates naturally, touching every aspect of operations and culture. The leader's approach to responsibility becomes a model for others, encouraging a culture of ownership and proactive problem-solving at all levels.

Blame in this context refers to that which happens inside and outside the organisation. The enlightened leader

Taoist Leadership: The Art of Subtle Influence

understands that the boundaries between internal and external factors are often blurred. They recognize that external challenges can have internal roots, and internal issues can manifest in external consequences. By accepting responsibility broadly, they gain a holistic view of the organization's place within its larger ecosystem.

They are able to foresee and avoid similar problems in the future. This foresight comes not from some mystical ability, but from the deep understanding that develops when one truly owns both successes and failures. By fully engaging with challenges, rather than avoiding them, the leader develops an intuitive grasp of systemic patterns and potential pitfalls.

The water-like quality of the enlightened leader also manifests in their approach to power. They don't seek to dominate or control but to support and nurture. Like water that provides essential sustenance to all life, these leaders create an environment where others can grow and thrive. They understand that their strength comes not from personal accolades or authority, but from the collective success of the entire organization.

Moreover, like water that can exist in multiple states - liquid, solid, or gas - the enlightened leader is versatile and adaptable. They can be firm when necessary, fluid when flexibility is required, and can even seem to disappear when their direct presence might hinder progress. This chameleon-like ability allows them to negotiate complex situations with grace and effectiveness.

The enlightened leader's acceptance of blame is not a sign of weakness, but a demonstration of strength and confidence.

Taoist Leadership: The Art of Subtle Influence

It shows a deep understanding that mistakes and setbacks are not just inevitable but are essential components of growth and learning. By embracing this reality, they create a culture where innovation can flourish, unhampered by fear of failure.

Ultimately, the enlightened leader who embodies these water-like qualities becomes a transformative force within their organization. They don't just manage or direct; they cultivate and catalyse. Like water that gradually shapes landscapes over time, these leaders shape their organizations not through forceful decrees, but through consistent, patient, and wise influence. Their legacy is not built on monuments to their own ego, but on the lasting positive changes they bring about in the people and structures around them.

Promoting Independence

Lao Tzu considered the ideal social grouping (at every level from family to nation) to be one in which every member can reach their potential in whichever direction that takes them. This profound insight recognizes that true flourishing occurs when individuals are given the freedom and support to pursue their unique paths. It's a vision of society that balances individual liberty with collective well-being, understanding that these two elements are not in opposition, but are mutually reinforcing.

They have access to health care, education and recreation. Nothing short of the pursuit of happiness. In this ideal, the basic needs of individuals are met not as an end in themselves, but as a means to enable higher pursuits. Health care ensures that physical and mental well-being are not barriers to personal growth. Education provides the tools and knowledge necessary for individuals to explore their interests and develop their talents. Recreation offers the space for rejuvenation and creative expression. Together, these elements form the foundation for what Lao Tzu saw as the ultimate aim of society: the pursuit of happiness.

Every person values their life, so they will value life-enhancing activities that they instinctively know is the way to find themselves, develop a strong sense of purpose and ultimately reach their full potential. This statement speaks to the innate drive within humans to seek meaning and self-actualization. When given the opportunity, people naturally gravitate towards activities that enrich their lives and bring them closer to understanding their place in the world. This process of self-discovery is not just personally fulfilling, but also contributes to the overall health and dynamism of the society.

When a person feels strong and independent they are likely to work hard, maintain good relationships and remain loyal to the organisation. Here, Lao Tzu touches on the paradoxical nature of true independence. When individuals feel empowered and self-reliant, they are more likely to form strong, positive connections with others and commit themselves wholeheartedly to their communities or organizations. This is because their engagement comes from a place of choice and alignment with their values, rather than from obligation or dependency.

This philosophy of promoting independence extends beyond just allowing freedom. It involves actively creating environments where independence can thrive. In a family context, this might mean parents encouraging their children to make decisions and learn from their mistakes. In a workplace, it could involve managers delegating authority and trusting employees to find innovative solutions. At a national level, it might manifest as policies that support entrepreneurship, lifelong learning, and social mobility.

The emphasis on independence doesn't mean isolation or selfishness. Rather, it fosters a type of interdependence where strong, self-reliant individuals come together to create resilient, adaptive communities. This approach recognizes that diverse, empowered individuals bring a wealth of perspectives and skills to collective endeavours, making the whole stronger than the sum of its parts.

Taoist Leadership: The Art of Subtle Influence

Moreover, this model of society is inherently dynamic and self-renewing. As individuals pursue their potential, they continually bring new ideas, skills, and energy into the social fabric. This creates a virtuous cycle where personal growth and societal progress are intertwined, each fuelling the other.

In essence, Lao Tzu's vision challenges us to rethink traditional top-down models of social organization. Instead of trying to control or direct people's lives, the wise leader or policymaker focuses on creating the conditions where independence can flourish. This approach requires trust in people's inherent capacity for growth and self-direction, as well as patience to allow natural processes of development to unfold.

Ultimately, promoting independence in this way leads to a society that is not just more fulfilling for its members, but also more innovative, resilient, and harmonious. It's a vision that remains deeply relevant today, offering a path to address many of the social and organizational challenges we face in our increasingly complex world.

Epilogue

These have been the principles of Taoist leadership, as outlined by Lao Tzu 3,500 years ago, principles that are as fresh and useful today as they have ever been.

Reflect on the path we've walked and the wisdom we've encountered. The concepts we've explored may seem paradoxical at first glance – leading by stepping back, influencing through non-action, and achieving more by doing less. Yet, these ideas have stood the test of time, offering a profound alternative to the often aggressive and ego-driven leadership styles prevalent in today's world.

Remember, the essence of Taoist leadership lies not in forceful control or loud proclamations, but in the subtle art of creating an environment where others can flourish. It's about becoming like water – fluid, adaptable, and capable of wearing away even the hardest obstacles over time. This approach requires patience, humility, and a deep understanding of human nature.

As you move forward from this book, consider how you might apply these principles in your daily life and leadership roles:

1. Cultivate simplicity in your actions and decisions.
2. Lead by example, allowing your consistent behaviour to inspire others.
3. Embrace humility, knowing that true strength often lies in gentleness.
4. Practice strategic non-action, recognizing when stepping back allows situations to resolve naturally.

5. Foster unity and collaboration, rather than competition within your team or organization.
6. Maintain integrity in all your dealings, building trust through consistent ethical behaviour.
7. Develop your intuition, learning to sense the underlying currents in any situation.

The path of Taoist leadership is not always easy. It requires us to set aside our ego, to resist the urge for immediate gratification or recognition. It challenges us to trust in processes we cannot always see or control. But the rewards – both personal and professional – can be profound.

As you implement these principles, you may find that your influence grows in unexpected ways. People may begin to seek out your guidance more often. Conflicts may resolve themselves with less intervention. Your team might become more cohesive and self-motivated. And you may discover a sense of ease and flow in your leadership that you hadn't thought possible.

Remember, becoming a Taoist leader is not about achieving perfection. It's about continuous growth, adaptation, and alignment with natural principles. There will be challenges and setbacks along the way. Embrace these as opportunities for learning and refinement.

I encourage you to revisit the concepts in this book regularly. Each reading may reveal new insights as your experiences and perspective evolve. Consider keeping a journal to reflect on your leadership journey, noting how these principles manifest in your life and work.

Finally, share these ideas with others. Not through preaching or forceful persuasion, but by embodying these principles in your actions. Let your leadership speak for itself, inspiring others to explore this path of subtle influence.

As Lao Tzu said, *"A leader is best when people barely know he exists, when his work is done, his aim fulfilled, they will say: we did it ourselves."* May you find the wisdom and courage to become such a leader, guiding with a gentle hand and a compassionate heart.

Thank you for embarking on this journey of Taoist leadership. May your path be filled with harmony, insight, and the quiet satisfaction of leadership well practiced. The way of subtle influence awaits – go forth and lead wisely.

About the Author

Taoist Leadership: The Art of Subtle Influence

David Tuffley PhD is a distinguished scholar of comparative religion and a dedicated follower of the Tao, bringing a unique blend of academic rigor and personal insight to his work. His journey in exploring the interconnections between various faith traditions and philosophical systems has spanned several decades, with a particular focus on the ancient wisdom of Taoism and its relevance in the modern world.

David's academic journey reached a significant milestone in 2008 with the successful completion of his PhD. His doctoral project, which culminated in the development of a Process Reference Model of leadership, represented a innovative approach to understanding and codifying the complex dynamics of effective leadership. This model, drawing from both Eastern and Western philosophical traditions, offers a comprehensive framework for analyzing and improving leadership practices across various organizational contexts.

Throughout his career, Dr. Tuffley has maintained a deep personal connection to the principles of Taoism, integrating its teachings of balance, simplicity, and harmony into both his academic work and personal life. This long-standing engagement with Taoist philosophy has provided him with a unique lens through which to view contemporary challenges in leadership, ethics, and personal development.

David's expertise extends beyond the confines of traditional academic research. He is known for his ability to bridge the gap between ancient wisdom and modern applications, offering insights that are both profound and practical. His work often explores how the timeless principles of Taoism and other Eastern philosophies can be applied to address the complexities of 21st-century life, from organizational management to personal well-being.

David's contributions to the field extend beyond the classroom and research papers. He is a prolific writer and speaker, sharing his insights through books, articles, and public lectures. His work often explores the intersections of technology, ethics, and spirituality, offering fresh perspectives on how ancient wisdom can guide us through the rapid changes of the digital age.

In addition to his academic pursuits, Dr. Tuffley is actively involved in community initiatives that promote cross-cultural understanding and interfaith dialogue. His background in comparative religion makes him a valuable facilitator in bringing together diverse groups to find common ground and foster mutual respect.

About the Author

David Tuffley PhD is an Australian scholar of comparative religion. exploring the fascinating range of diverse faiths and belief systems through a lens of academic rigor and cultural sensitivity.

Visit David's Websites:

http://altiorapublications.com/

https://experts.griffith.edu.au/8010-david-tuffley

https://www.facebook.com/tuffley/

https://theconversation.com/profiles/david-tuffley-13731

Other books by David Tuffley

David is the author of 70+ non-fiction books on a wide range of subjects. To view the latest list of books, or google/search on: **tuffley amazon books**

One last thing...

If you found this work instructive, I'd be very grateful if you'd post a short review on Amazon or wherever you bought it. Your support really does make a difference and I read all the reviews personally so I can get your feedback and make this book even better.

Thanks again for your support!

David Tuffley

Notes

Notes

Notes

Notes

Notes

Notes

Notes

Notes

Notes

Notes

Notes

Notes

Notes

Notes

Notes

Notes

Notes

Notes

Notes

Notes

Notes

www.ingramcontent.com/pod-product-compliance
Lightning Source LLC
Chambersburg PA
CBHW070419220526
45466CB00004B/1462

HR is Sexy

Revolutionizing Human Resources

NICOLE ANDERSON

Cover design and interior formatting by:
King's Custom Covers
www.KingsCustomCovers.com

HR is Sexy Copyright © 2021 Nicole Anderson and MEND Publishing. All rights reserved. Printed in the United States of America. No part of this book may be used or reproduced in any manner whatsoever without written permission except in the case of brief quotations embodied in critical articles or reviews.

For more information please contact MEND HR at: HRAnswers@MENDHR.com

ISBN: 979-8533809801

First Edition: August 2021

10 9 8 7 6 5 4 3 2 1